hen

gallina

rooster

gallo

chick

pollito

duckling

patito

turkey

pavo

donkey

burro

swan

cisne

frog

rana

racoon

mapache

bear

oso

squirrel

ardilla

fly

mosca

ladybug

mariquita

worm

gusano

snail

caracol

slug

babosa

bee

abeja

spider

araña

beetle

escarabajo

dragonfly

libélula

lion

león

zebra

cebra

giraffe

jirafa

rhinoceros

rinoceronte

snake

serpiente

mosquito

mosquito

sea turtle

tortuga marina

hippopotamus

hipopótamo

alligator

caimán

crocodile

cocodrilo

shark

tiburón

walrus

morsa

penguin

pingüino

polar bear

oso polar

seal

foca

starfish

estrella de mar

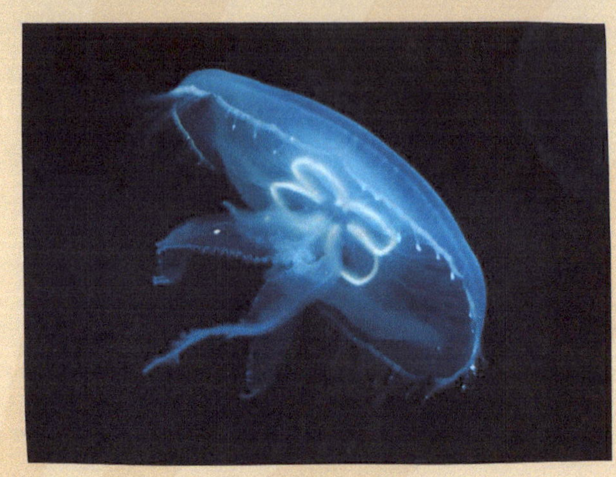

jellyfish

medusa

seashells

conchas marinas

feather

pluma

11

eleven

once

12

twelve

doce

13

thirteen

trece

14

fourteen

catorce

15

fifteen

quince

16

sixteen

dieciséis

17

seventeen

diecisiete

18

eighteen

dieciocho

19

nineteen

diecinueve

20

twenty

veinte

heart

corazón

oval

óvalo

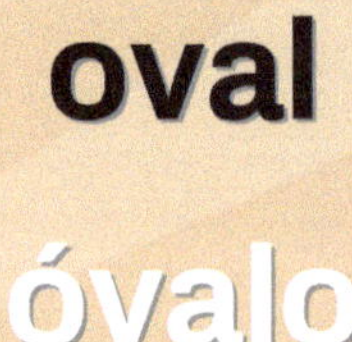

arrow

flecha

crescent

creciente

curve

curva

spiral

espiral

cross

cruz

zigzag

zigzag

rainbow

arcoíris

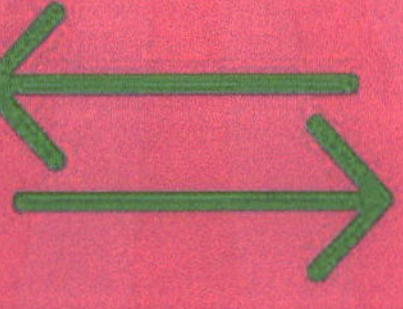

dark colors

colores oscuros

light colors

colores claros

dots

puntos

line

línea

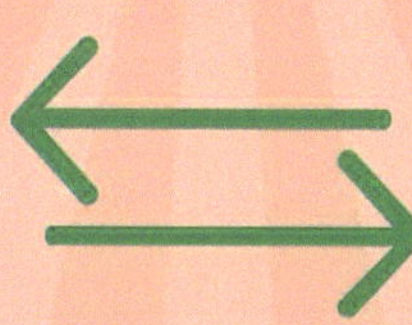

short

bajo

tall

alto

 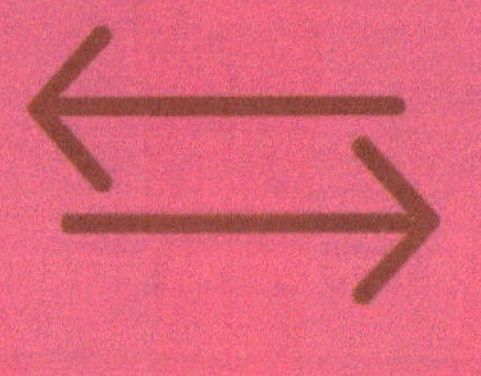 

a little

un poco

a lot

mucho

full

lleno

empty

vacío

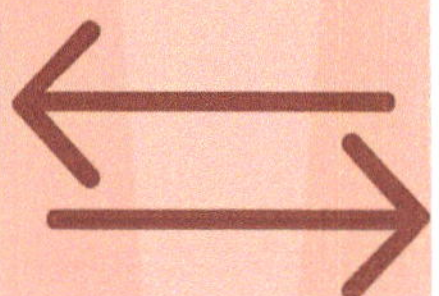

curly hair

cabello rizado

straight hair

cabello liso

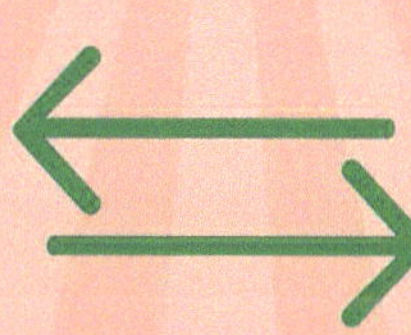

accept

aceptar

refuse

rechazar

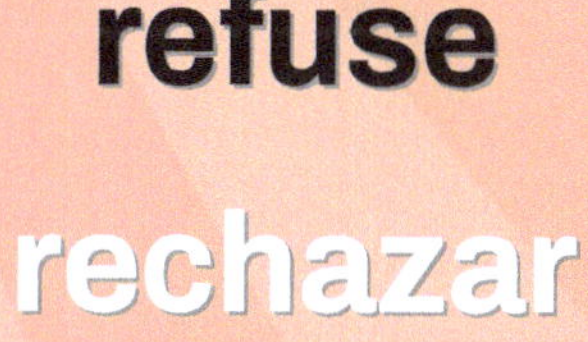

identical

idéntico

different

diferente

dry

seco

wet

mojado

toys

juguetes

blocks

bloques

ball

pelota

robots

robots

tongue

lengua

nose

nariz

hair

cabello

moustache

bigote

fingers

dedos

arm

brazo

knee

rodilla

elbow

codo

smile

sonreír

kiss

beso

cry

llorar

pain

dolor

body

cuerpo

back

espalda

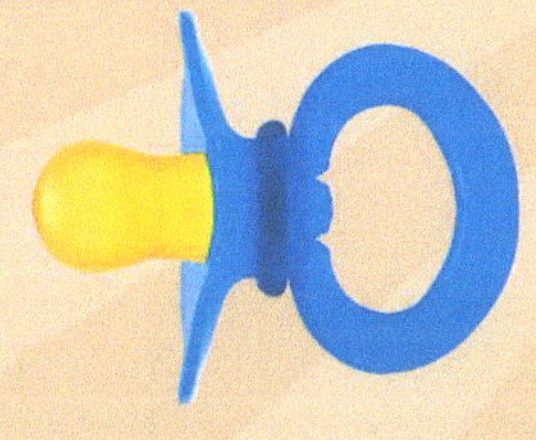

pacifier

chupete

high chair

trona

soap

jabón

toothbrush

cepillo de dientes

towel

toalla

potty

orinal

ring

anillo

bracelet

pulsera

necklace

collar

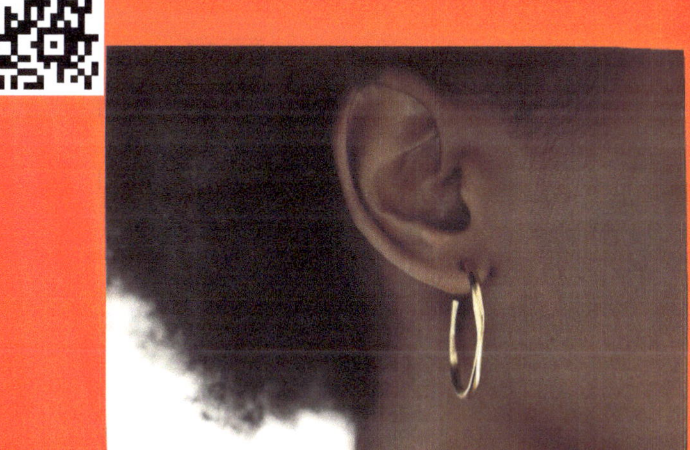

earring

pendiente

chocolate

chocolate

popcorn

palomitas

jam

mermelada

toast

tostada

honey

miel

butter

mantequilla

bread

pan

ice cream

helado

semolina

sémola

rice

arroz

pasta

pasta

soup

sopa

milk

leche

water

agua

juice

zumo

kiwi

kiwi

raspberry

frambuesa

grapefruit

pomelo

melon

melón

plum

ciruela

apricot

albaricoque

pomegranate

granada

fig

higo

blueberry

arándano

cranberry

arándano

persimmon

caqui

lychee

lichi

fruits

frutas

vegetables

verduras

avocado

aguacate

green bean

judía verde

broccoli

brócoli

eggplant

berenjena

peas

guisantes

bell pepper

pimiento

beet

remolacha

lettuce

lechuga

endive

endivia

artichoke

alcachofa

leek

puerro

onion

cebolla

garlic

ajo

ginger

jengibre

walnuts

nueces

almond

almendra

pistachio

pistacho

cashew

anacardo